essentials
CHOCOLATE

essentials
CHOCOLATE

Exploit the versatility, aroma and taste

Edited by Jane Donovan

APPLE

With much love to Gary Connell and thanks for his culinary inspiration

A QUINTET BOOK

Published by the Apple Press
6 Blundell Street
London N7 9BH

ISBN 1-84092-217-6

This book was designed and produced by
Quintet Publishing Limited
6 Blundell Street
London N7 9BH

Creative Director: Richard Dewing
Art Director: Paula Marchant
Designer: Isobel Gillan
Senior Editor: Clare Hubbard
Assistant Editor: Carine Tracanelli
Editor: Jane Donovan

Typeset in Great Britain by
Central Southern Typesetters, Eastbourne
Manufactured in Hong Kong by
Regent Publishing Services Ltd
Printed in China by
Leefung-Asco Printers Ltd

Material in this book has previously appeared in Quintet titles.

Note:
Because of the risk of salmonella poisoning, raw eggs should not be served to the very young, the ill or elderly, or to pregnant women.

If using an ice-cream machine always refer to the manufacturer's instructions regarding capacity and operation.

Titles also available in this series are *Tomato* (ISBN 1-84092-219-2) and *Egg* (ISBN 1-84092-218-4).

CONTENTS

Introduction

chocolate

is an ingredient which is enjoyed the world over.

It was first discovered by the **adventurous**

conquistador, Hernán Cortés, who landed on the coast of Vera

Cruz in 1519. On reaching the Aztec capital, Tenochtitlán, Cortés was

intrigued by the Aztecs' consumption of a strange brew known as *xocolatl* (the first

drinking chocolate) and he introduced his own, sweeter version to the court

of King Charles V. Today chocolate is available in more luxurious forms, including

dark, couverture, Grand Cru, white, and semisweet, yet it still has the same seductive qualities.

Chocolate needs to be stored away from light, moisture, and strong scents in a room with a maximum

humidity of 65 percent. Good dark chocolate can keep for at least one and a half years in these conditions and although

white and semisweet chocolate will not last as long, they too are surprisingly robust. If **chocolate** is

kept in the refrigerator or freezer it must be stored in a wrapped airtight container. Open the package at

room temperature. Warm and **comforting,** chocolate can actually trigger off similar

feelings to those experienced when people fall in love. It is an essential ingredient as it can be

used to create so many delicious drinks, ice creams, instant **sauces,**

garnishes and desserts. Cocoa, chocolate spreads and pastes are also excellent

store cupboard stand-bys. Keep a selection of **good-**

quality chocolate and chocolate products in your

kitchen, experiment with the recipes and ideas in this

book and enjoy chocolate

at its finest.

The flavors of chocolate

Entirely natural, chocolate is loaded with many different compounds and only becomes edible after a long and involved process that includes fermentation. In cooking, aim to use chocolate with a high percentage of cocoa for the best results and purchase different types of chocolate to vary flavour and textures. Shown here are some popular varieties of dark and semisweet chocolate:

2

2 **couverture** is the French term for chocolate used by chocolatiers and pastry chefs as one of their raw materials. It is used to achieve a high gloss when tempering chocolate and renowned for its ready melting qualities and workability.

dark chocolate
has a substantially higher cocoa content and whatever beans are used they will be unlikely to make much impression through the sweetness of this chocolate.

I

grand cru
is a term coined by the French company Valrhona in 1986 for their Guanaja dark chocolate couverture that uses only South American beans. Beware of cheap imitations. There are also some semisweet Grand Crus but these are really blends of rare cocoa.

₃ semisweet chocolate
most closely reflects each individual country's chocolate tastes.

3

Specialist **chocolate** products

*C*hocolate products, organic chocolate and white chocolate are all essential ingredients to have at hand in the kitchen. Some may need to be refrigerated once open, so follow the manufacturer's advice. They can be used to make different sauces, instant snacks and quick desserts (for example, try coating sections of fresh fruit with various types of chocolate to balance the acidity of the fruit). Shown here are some useful products and varieties of chocolate:

4

4 chocolate sauce is a great accompaniment to ice creams and desserts.

₁ chocolate spread (some include nuts or alcohol) can be used to enliven crêpes, muffins and all kinds of snacks.

1

₂ cocoa (always use the best quality) adds flavour to all kinds of recipes and is great for garnishing.

2

3

₃ white chocolate is a combination of cocoa butter, sugar and milk. Avoid over-sweet varieties and look for a good clean break.

6

5

₅ chocolate chips can be used as a garnish or added to ice creams, cakes and cookies.

₆ confectionery —literally thousands of sweets have chocolate as a flavouring or coating. Chocolate-coated coffee beans are shown here.

Cooking Techniques

Before you begin any of the recipes in this book, try working with chocolate first. Learn how to melt chocolate and experiment with some simple garnishes.

Melting Chocolate

This is an easy technique but you must avoid overheating chocolate or it will turn into a mass of lumps. The same thing happens if you accidentally drop water into hot melted chocolate.

Break the chocolate into squares and place it in a heatproof bowl. Add any liquid flavourings such as liqueurs or coffee, or chopped nuts or dried fruits.

Set the bowl over a heavy saucepan of gently simmering water. Ensure the base of the bowl is not touching the water at any time during the melting process. Stir occasionally and remove the bowl from the heat as soon as the chocolate has melted.

To microwave chocolate, break it up into squares and place in a bowl with flavourings as desired (see above). Microwave in short bursts of 30 seconds on the lowest setting, stirring between each one, until melted.

Chocolate-dipped Fruits

Just about any fresh or dried fruit can be dipped in chocolate. Use pure, melted chocolate and serve the same day as a light dessert, or use as a garnish.

About 12 pieces of fruit (try strawberries, cherries, grapes, orange segments, dates, dried apricots or other dried fruits and lychees)
125 g (4½ oz) fine-quality white chocolate, chopped
3 squares dark or semisweet chocolate, chopped

Clean and prepare the fruits. Wipe strawberries with a soft cloth; wash and dry firm-skinned fruits such as cherries and grapes. Dry well and set on kitchen paper to absorb excess moisture.

Line a baking sheet with greaseproof paper. Melt the white chocolate (see page 12). Holding the fruits by the stem or end and at an angle, dip about two-thirds of the fruit into the chocolate. Allow the excess to drip off and place on the baking sheet. Continue dipping fruits and if the chocolate becomes too thick, set it over hot water again briefly to soften slightly.

Refrigerate the fruits until the chocolate sets, about 20 minutes, then melt the dark or semisweet chocolate (see page 12). Dip the tip of each fruit into the melted chocolate and set on the baking sheet again. Refrigerate until set, about 15 minutes. To serve, remove from the refrigerator 10 to 15 minutes in advance.

Chocolate Leaves

Use firm non-toxic leaves with clearly defined veins, such as rose or bay, for this chocolate decoration. Wash and dry the leaves before use. Leaves can also be made with melted semisweet or white chocolate but neither sets as well as dark chocolate.

Melt a large bar of dark chocolate (see page 12). Hold the leaves by the stalks and draw them, veined side down, over the surface of the melted chocolate. Alternatively, use a pastry or clean artist's brush to coat the leaf. Wipe off any chocolate that may have run onto the front of the leaf. Lay the leaves out on a plate to allow the chocolate to set. Once the chocolate is firm, peel away the real leaves to reveal chocolate replicas.

Chocolate Garnishes

• Dust the edges of cakes and pastries with sieved cocoa powder or sieve cocoa powder directly through a doily.

• Dip cigarettes russes or other delicate biscuits in melted chocolate and serve with ice creams and sorbets.

• Swirl melted chocolate (see page 12) onto a worktop or marble chopping board in a variety of different shapes. Leave to set and remove with a palette knife. These decorations can be made in advance, then stored in airtight containers until needed.

• Try shredding chocolate with a grater for an instant garnish for drinks, cakes and desserts. Experiment with different textures.

Chocolate Curls

A quick and easy way to make an attractive decoration with chocolate.

450 g (1 lb) cooking chocolate

Break the chocolate into pieces and melt it in a bowl over hot water (see page 12). Spread it out thickly on a sheet of greaseproof paper and allow to set completely.

Using a vegetable peeler, gently take curls from the chocolate and serve them with a whole range of desserts.

Drink Toppings

Chocolate and cocoa can be used to make all kinds of quick toppings for drinks. Try some of the following ideas:

• Make a classic cappuccino and dust with good-quality sieved cocoa powder.
• Dip tiny marshmallows into melted chocolate (see page 12) and serve with hot chocolate or malty shakes.
• Dip the edge of the glass into cocoa powder, then grate chocolate over milk shakes and serve immediately.

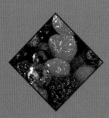 # THE BASICS

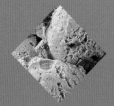

Chocolate Sauce

This delicious sauce is excellent served as an accompaniment to all kinds of desserts.

MAKES **280** ML (½ PINT)

225 g (8 oz) dark chocolate
2 Tbsp butter
6 Tbsp milk
½ tsp vanilla extract

Break the chocolate into small pieces and place in a small bowl. Melt over a heavy saucepan of simmering water (see page 12). Add the butter, milk and vanilla extract.

Stir the sauce until smooth, then serve warm.

Tip

• *If liked, substitute half the milk with single cream or brandy, rum, Tia Maria or sherry. For a thinner sauce, add an extra 2 tablespoons milk.*

Chocolate Orange Sauce

Evaporated milk can be used in place of cream, if preferred.

MAKES ABOUT **280** ML (½ PINT)

225 g (8 oz) dark chocolate (use chips or a bar
  broken into small squares)

4 Tbsp golden syrup

1 Tbsp butter

160 ml (6 fl oz) single cream

1 orange, grated zest and juice

2 to 3 Tbsp orange liqueur, e.g. Cointreau

This sauce may be made in a microwave or in a bowl set over a heavy saucepan of hot water. Heat the chocolate, golden syrup and butter together until melted. Stir in the cream and whisk until thoroughly mixed.

Stir in the orange zest and juice, then the liqueur and serve as desired.

Chocolate Syrup

This is a useful topping sauce for sponge cakes and frozen desserts.

SERVES **3** TO **4**

450 g (1 lb) light brown sugar
120 g (4½ oz) cocoa powder
280 ml (½ pt) boiling water
2 tsp vanilla extract

In a bowl, mix together the sugar and cocoa powder. Add the water, stirring continuously.

Transfer the mixture to a small heavy saucepan and simmer gently for 10 minutes, stirring frequently. Allow to cool, then add the vanilla extract.

Cover and chill in the refrigerator.

Hot Chocolate Fudge

A very quick and easy sauce, which must be used right away because it thickens in the refrigerator.

SERVES **3** TO **4**

250 g (9 oz) good dark chocolate, broken into small
    pieces
3 Tbsp golden syrup
1 tsp coffee essence (optional)
6 Tbsp hot water

Heat the chocolate, syrup and coffee essence together in a heavy saucepan until the chocolate has melted. Stir in the hot water, then remove from the heat. Beat thoroughly for a few seconds until smooth.

Bittersweet Chocolate

Two different types of chocolate in a creamy sauce sweetened with a little honey makes a wonderful bittersweet chocolate topping.

SERVES **3** TO **4**

8 Tbsp single cream
2 Tbsp clear honey
85 g (3 oz) fine dark chocolate, finely chopped
85 g (3 oz) semisweet chocolate, finely chopped
1 tsp unsalted butter
½ tsp vanilla extract

Heat the cream and honey gently together until blended. Add the chocolate and butter. Continue stirring over a low heat until the chocolate has melted and all the ingredients are combined. Add the vanilla, then serve the sauce warm.

Chocolate Pastry

This is a wonderfully rich, sweet pastry, almost like a chocolate biscuit. It makes a stunning background for fruit tarts and tartlets, as well as chocolate fillings.

MAKES ENOUGH TO COVER A **23** TO **25**-CM
  (**9** TO **10**-INCH) TART DISH.

110 g (4 oz) unsalted butter, softened
70 g (2½ oz) caster sugar

½ tsp salt
2 tsp vanilla extract
85 g (3 oz) cocoa powder (preferably Dutch
  processed)
225 g (8 oz) plain flour

Put the butter, sugar, salt and vanilla into the bowl of a food processor fitted with the metal blade; process for 25 to 30 seconds until creamy, scraping down the sides of the bowl when necessary. Add the cocoa. Process about 1 minute until well blended. Add the flour all at once and, using the pulse button, process for 10 to 15 seconds until the flour is well blended. Scrape the pastry out onto a sheet of clingfilm and shape into a flat circle. Wrap and refrigerate.

Soften the pastry for 10 to 15 minutes at room temperature. Unwrap the pastry and sandwich between two large pieces of clingfilm. Carefully roll out to about a 27-cm (11-inch) round, about 6-mm (¼-inch) thick. Peel off the top sheet of clingfilm and invert the pastry into a greased tart dish. Ease the pastry onto the base and sides of the pan, then remove the second layer of clingfilm. Press the pastry onto the base and sides of the pan, then roll the rolling pin over the top of the pan to cut off any excess pastry. Prick the base of the pastry with a fork and refrigerate 1 hour.

Preheat an oven to 200°C/400°F/Gas 6. Blind bake the tart (line pastry case with greaseproof paper or foil, then fill with dried beans, rice or pastry weights) for 10 minutes. Remove the paper, foil or beans and continue baking for 5 more minutes just until set. Transfer to a wire rack to cool completely.

Ganache & Berry Tart

Summer berries make a perfect match for a rich chocolate tart case filled with a dark chocolate and raspberry truffle mixture.

SERVES **6** TO **8**

570 ml (1 pt) double cream
230 g (8 oz) seedless raspberry jam
250 g (9 oz) good-quality dark chocolate, chopped

1 chocolate pastry tart (see page 22)
4 Tbsp framboise or other fruit-flavoured liqueur
680 g (1½ lb) mixed fresh summer berries
1 to 2 Tbsp caster sugar

In a heavy saucepan over medium heat, bring 340 ml (12 fl oz) of the cream and three-quarters of the jam to the boil, whisking to dissolve the jam. Remove from the heat and add the chocolate all at once, stirring until melted and smooth. Strain the mixture directly into the tart shell, lifting and turning the tart to distribute the filling evenly. Cool completely or refrigerate until set, at least 1 hour.

In a small heavy saucepan over medium heat, heat the remaining raspberry jam and 2 tablespoons liqueur until melted and bubbling. Place the berries in a bowl and drizzle over the syrup; toss to coat well. Arrange the berries on top of the tart and refrigerate until ready to serve.

To serve, bring the tart to room temperature at least 30 minutes before serving. Whip the remaining cream with the sugar and remaining liqueur until soft peaks form. Spoon into a serving bowl and serve with the tart.

Chocolate Truffles

These delicious truffles are made from a ganache base. They can be rolled in cocoa or finely chopped nuts, or dipped in chocolate.

MAKES ABOUT **24**

230 ml (8 fl oz) double cream
340 g (12 oz) good-quality dark chocolate, chopped
2 Tbsp unsalted butter
2 Tbsp brandy or other favourite liqueur

COATING
Cocoa powder or 450 g (1 lb) dark chocolate

In a heavy saucepan bring the cream to the boil. Remove from the heat and add all the chocolate, stirring until melted and smooth. Beat in the butter until melted and stir in the liqueur. Strain into a bowl and cool to room temperature. Refrigerate until thickened and firm, about 2 hours.

Line a baking sheet with greaseproof paper. With a teaspoon, form the mixture into small balls and place on the prepared baking sheet.

If dusting with cocoa, sieve about 55 g (2 oz) cocoa into a small bowl. Drop each ball into the cocoa; toss with a fork to coat, then roll lightly between the palms of your hands, rounding the balls. (Dust your hands with cocoa first to prevent the truffles from sticking.) Do not worry if the truffles are not perfectly round as an irregular shape is more authentic.

Shake the cocoa-coated truffles in a sieve to remove excess cocoa. Refrigerate, covered, in an airtight container for up to 2 weeks, or freeze for up to 2 months. Soften slightly at room temperature before serving.

If coating with melted chocolate, do not roll in cocoa, but freeze for 2 hours after forming into balls. Melt the chocolate in a small bowl (see page 12) and, using a fork, dip the balls into the melted chocolate one at a time, tapping the fork on the side of the bowl to shake off excess chocolate. Place on a prepared baking sheet and refrigerate immediately to keep the coating shiny. (If the melted chocolate thickens, reheat gently to thin.)

 # SHAKES & SODAS

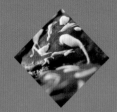

Chocolate Truffle

The chocolate complements the coffee flavour very well.

MAKES 1 LARGE SERVING

230 ml (8 fl oz) strong chocolate truffle-flavoured
    coffee, chilled
8 Tbsp whole milk
1 scoop vanilla ice cream
Ice
½ to 2 tsp coffee syrup or sugar
Whipped cream and grated chocolate, to serve

Place the coffee, milk and ice cream in the blender. Process until smoth. Pour into a glass with a little ice and sweeten to taste with coffee syrup or sugar. Top with a swirl of whipped cream and garnish with grated chocolate.

Chocolate Shake

Simple, rich and delicious, this is the ultimate chocolate shake.

MAKES I LARGE SERVING

I cup whole milk
I scoop chocolate ice cream

Place the milk and ice cream in the blender. Process until smooth. Pour into a glass and top with one of the options given below.

Chocolate Shake Toppings

Top your basic chocolate shake with any of the following, used alone or in combination:
- *Whipping cream.*
- *An extra scoop of ice cream: try vanilla, white chocolate, raspberry, macadamia, pecan, chocolate chip or almond.*
- *Sauces: chocolate, strawberry, butterscotch or fudge are really good over an extra scoop of ice cream. Liqueurs are great too.*
- *Chocolate chips, candies, vermicelli or breakfast cereals.*
- *Spices: try cinnamon, nutmeg or apple pie spices.*
- *Toasted nuts: try pecans, almonds, hazelnuts or macadamias.*

Chocolate Shake Variations

- Stir 2 tablespoons dark chocolate chunks or chips into the blended mixture by hand. Add white chocolate chips for a change.
- Add 2 tablespoons brandy, Cointreau, Amaretto or Irish Cream to the chocolate chip mixture described above.
- Stir in by hand two to three crushed after-dinner mints.
- Substitute up to 6 tablespoons single cream for the milk.
- Stir one large or two to three small cookies into the shake by hand. Drink this shake quickly or the crunch will disappear from the cookies. Try chocolate chip or chocolate orange cookies.
- Add up to 4 tablespoons crunchy peanut butter with the ice cream.
- Try 2 tablespoons mini marshmallows and 2 tablespoons chopped mixed nuts, and top with more of the same.
- Add up to 1 tablespoon natural almond syrup or a few drops of natural almond extract.
- Chop one small banana and add it in at the same time as the cream and milk.
- Stir 340 g (12 ounces) chopped fresh strawberries into the shake by hand. Top with strawberry sauce and toasted coconut. Other fruits, such as raspberries and peaches, are good too.
- Add 3 tablespoons crushed praline. Top with an extra spoonful.

Caramel Chocolate Bar

Caramel chocolate bar ice creams are very popular. The ones prepared in ice cream parlours can be used in shakes, but those that are individually wrapped and sold in a supermarket do not make successful shakes. Try this home-made version. It does not contain a bar, but has all the indulgent ingredients.

MAKES I LARGE SERVING

8 Tbsp whole milk
I scoop rich chocolate ice cream
I scoop vanilla ice cream
I Tbsp butterscotch sauce
2 Tbsp dark chocolate chips
I scoop vanilla ice cream, butterscotch sauce
  and chopped, toasted peanuts or almonds,
  for the topping

Blend together the milk, ice creams and butterscotch sauce. Pour into a glass, then stir in the chocolate chips by hand. Top with more vanilla ice cream and drizzle over plenty of butterscotch sauce. Sprinkle with chopped nuts. You can even go one step further and decorate the glass with a caramel star!

Mocha Shake

In this recipe the coffee tempers the sweetness of the chocolate.

MAKES I LARGE SERVING

170 ml (6 fl oz) whole milk
4 Tbsp strong coffee
2 scoops chocolate ice cream
Whipped cream, chocolate-coated coffee beans
  or grated chocolate, to decorate

Place all the ingredients in a blender and process until smooth. Top with whipped cream and decorate.

Brown Cow

This traditional recipe has never lost its appeal.

MAKES 1 LARGE SERVING

1 Tbsp chocolate syrup (purchased or see page 19)
2 scoops vanilla ice cream
Cola
Whipped cream and maraschino cherry, for
 the topping

Place the syrup and one scoop of ice cream in the bottom of a tall glass with a little cola. Stir and add sufficient cola to fill the glass three-quarters full. Add the second scoop of ice cream, then top up the glass with more cola. Top with cream and finish with a cherry.

Advice on Soda-making

- *It is important to rest the ice cream in the refrigerator for 15 to 20 minutes before making sodas (or shakes) otherwise the initial mixing of the syrup, juice or drink will not include the creaminess of the ice cream. If you don't have time, pop the ice cream in the microwave for a few seconds to melt slightly.*

Double Chocolate Shake

Chocolate milk can be purchased or made at home from a chocolate syrup which can be mixed cold. Hot milk drinks form a skin and tend to come out of the solution when chilled. Cover with clingfilm to prevent a skin from forming and stir well before adding to the blender.

MAKES 1 LARGE SERVING

1 cup chocolate milk
2 scoops chocolate ice cream

Place the milk and the ice cream in the blender and process until smooth. Pour into a glass and top with one of the options (see page 28).

Choconana Milk Shake

This delicious shake combines everybody's favourite fruit – banana – with the great taste of chocolate.

SERVES 2 TO 3

280 ml (½ pt) milk
3 Tbsp chocolate syrup (purchased or see page 19)
700 ml (1¼ pt) chocolate ice cream
1 banana, cut into pieces
Chocolate flake bars, to serve

Put the milk, chocolate syrup, ice cream and banana into a blender. Cover and blend until smooth.

To serve, pour into glasses and add a chocolate flake to each one.

Hot Chocolate Float

Hot Chocolate Float

The ultimate comfort drink, it is always a pick-me-up on a cold day.

MAKES **4** SERVINGS

55 g (2 oz) chocolate chips
3 Tbsp sugar
280 ml (½ pt) water
450 ml (16 fl oz) whole milk
8 Tbsp single cream
½ tsp vanilla extract
4 scoops vanilla ice cream
Drinking chocolate or ground cinnamon, to decorate

Place the chocolate chips, sugar and water in a heavy saucepan and slowly bring to the boil. Boil, stirring constantly, for 2 minutes. Stir in the milk, cream and vanilla; heat through (do not boil). Beat with a wire whisk until frothy, then pour into four warmed mugs.

Carefully place a scoop of ice cream into each mug. Sprinkle with drinking chocolate or cinnamon and serve immediately.

Mocha Liqueur Cocktail

There are so many recipes for coffee and chocolate liqueurs, but this is simply wonderful. Add whipped cream as a topping if you feel self-indulgent.

SERVES **2**

2 Tbsp cocoa powder or flaked drinking chocolate
1 or 2 tsp light brown sugar
230 ml (8 fl oz) whole milk
230 ml (8 fl oz) strong hot coffee
4 Tbsp brandy
1 Tbsp finely grated chocolate

Blend the cocoa with the sugar and a little milk. Put the remaining milk in a small pan and bring almost to the boil. Pour the hot milk onto the paste and stir until smooth and blended. Return the cocoa to the pan with the hot coffee and heat gently until very hot but not boiling.

Pour into large mugs and add 2 tablespoons of brandy to each. Top with finely grated chocolate and serve immediately.

Old-fashioned Chocolate Soda

*Chocolate, chocolate, chocolate—
this is maybe the best-known and best-
loved soda.*

MAKES 1 LARGE SERVING

1 to 2 Tbsp chocolate syrup
  (see page 19)
1 Tbsp ice cream or double cream, whipped
Soda water
2 scoops chocolate ice cream
Whipped cream and grated chocolate, for the topping

Place the chocolate syrup in the bottom of a tall soda glass, then add the ice cream or double cream. Fill the glass three-quarters full with soda water; stir. Add the ice cream and top off the glass with more soda.

Top with whipped cream and grated chocolate. Serve with a long-handled spoon and a straw.

Variations

- *Chocolate Almond Syrup: add 1 tablespoon almond syrup.*
- *Chocolate Malt Soda: substitute chocolate malt syrup for the simple chocolate syrup.*

36

LITTLE TREATS

Chocolate Frosted Hearts

These biscuits taste delicious and look good too – a great Valentine's gift.

MAKES ABOUT **45**

8 Tbsp slightly salted butter, softened

70 g (2½ oz) brown sugar

170 ml (6 fl oz) molasses

1 tsp ground ginger

1 tsp cinnamon

½ tsp ground cloves

1 tsp baking soda

1 egg, beaten

560 g (1¼ lb) plain flour

DECORATION

110 g (4 oz) icing sugar

2 Tbsp unsweetened cocoa powder

1 egg white (see page 4)

Preheat an oven to 170°C/325°F/Gas 3. Grease two baking sheets. Cut the butter into pieces and place in a large bowl. Place the sugar, molasses and spices in a heavy saucepan and bring to the boil. Add the baking soda and pour into the bowl with the butter. Stir until the butter has melted, then stir in the egg. Sieve in the flour and mix until combined. Chill the dough until firm enough to roll out, about 1 hour.

Roll out on a lightly floured surface to 6-mm (¼-inch) thick. Cut into heart shapes with a 7.5-mm (3-inch) cutter. Place onto baking sheets and bake for 8 to 10 minutes. Transfer to a wire rack to cool.

Sieve the icing sugar and cocoa into a bowl. Beat in the egg white and continue beating until a soft peak consistency is reached. Spoon frosting onto the biscuits to cover and decorate. Return to the wire rack to set. Once set, store in an airtight container.

Decorating Ideas

These biscuits can be decorated in different ways depending upon the occasion:
- *Sugar strands or sugar crystals.*
- *Silver and gold dragées.*
- *Chopped nuts.*
- *Chocolate chunks.*
- *For Valentine's Day—spell out a name on the biscuits with frosting.*

White Chocolate & Toffee Swirl Fondue

White chocolate with a high percentage of cocoa butter works best for this recipe.

SERVES **6** TO **8**

225 g (8 oz) white chocolate
160 ml (6 fl oz) double cream
2 Tbsp demerara sugar

1 Tbsp golden syrup
2 Tbsp butter
2 Tbsp single cream

Break the chocolate into small pieces and place in the fondue pot with the double cream. Place over a moderate heat and cook gently, stirring frequently, until the chocolate has melted and is smooth and creamy. Carefully transfer to the lit burner.

Place the sugar, golden syrup and butter in a small pan and heat gently until blended. Remove from the heat and stir in the single cream.

Carefully pour the toffee sauce on top of the white chocolate fondue in a swirl. Serve with fresh fruit wedges, biscuits or pieces of sponge cake for dipping.

Velvety Chocolate Fondue

This decadent fondue is absolute heaven on earth! Like all dessert fondues, it can be prepared in the pot and then used without placing it over a burner: this will make the fondue even more luscious because it thickens as it cools so you get more chocolate each time you dip.

SERVES **6** TO **8**

225 g (8 oz) semisweet baking chocolate
230 ml (8 fl oz) double cream
3 to 4 Tbsp rum or Cointreau
1 Tbsp brown sugar (optional)

Break the chocolate into small pieces into the fondue pot. Pour in the cream, rum or Cointreau and sugar (if using). Place over a moderate heat and cook, stirring frequently, until melted and thoroughly blended.

Carefully transfer the fondue pot to the lit burner and serve.

Serving Ideas

- *Amaretti, chocolate chip cookies, shortbread, fresh strawberries and banana pieces speared onto fondue forks are all great dipping foods.*

Monkey Puzzles

These cookies are really rich and chocolatey, and lovely with a cup of coffee.

MAKES ABOUT 14

85 g (3 oz) plain flour
1½ Tbsp unsweetened cocoa powder
¼ tsp baking powder
85 g (3 oz) slightly salted butter, softened
6 Tbsp golden syrup
10 g (⅓ oz) bran flakes, coarsely crushed
250 g (9 oz) semisweet chocolate, coarsely chopped

Preheat an oven to 180°C/350°F/Gas 4. Grease two baking sheets. Sieve the flour, cocoa and baking powder into a bowl. Beat together the butter and golden syrup until soft. Stir in the flour mixture and mix until combined. Then stir in the bran flakes until well blended.

Place spoonfuls of the mixture spaced apart onto the baking sheets. Bake for 10 minutes. Transfer to a wire rack to cool.

Melt the chocolate in a bowl set over a heavy saucepan of barely simmering water (see page 12). When the cookies are completely cold, spread spoonfuls of melted chocolate over the top of them, then return to the wire rack to set. Once set, store in an airtight container.

Chocolate Cookie Ice Cream

An everyday family favourite.

SERVES **4** TO **6**

4 large egg yolks (see page 4)
70 g (2½ oz) caster sugar
280 ml (½ pt) milk
1 tsp vanilla extract
280 ml (½ pt) double cream
Two 55 g (2 oz) chocolate wafers coarsely chopped

First make the basic ice cream mixture. Using a fork, whisk the egg yolks and sugar together until thick and pale. Heat the milk until almost boiling, then pour it onto the eggs, stirring all the time with a wooden spoon. Return the mixture to the heavy saucepan and heat gently, stirring continuously, until the custard coats the back of the spoon—do not cook for too long or the eggs will scramble.

Transfer to a clean bowl and leave the mixture to cool, then stir in the vanilla and unbeaten cream. Chill thoroughly for at least one hour. Spoon or scrape the mixture into the ice-cream machine, freeze-churn until ready to serve, then add the chopped wafers. Continue churning until ready to serve.

Hazelnut Chocolate Crescents

These delicious nutty shortbread crescents can be dipped or drizzled with chocolate. They make a lovely Christmas biscuit.

MAKES **24**

110 g (4 oz) hazelnuts, unskinned
85 g (3 oz) semisweet chocolate, coarsely chopped, then halved
4 Tbsp granulated sugar
170 g (6 oz) plain flour
Pinch of salt
4 Tbsp butter

Preheat an oven to 180°C/350°F/Gas 4. Spread the hazelnuts on a baking sheet. Toast for 12 to 15 minutes until lightly browned. Leave to cool completely.

Melt half the chocolate in a small bowl over a heavy saucepan of barely simmering water (see page 12). Remove and set aside to cool. Process the nuts and 1 tablespoon of sugar in a food processor until fine; do not overprocess. Transfer to a medium bowl with the flour and salt. Beat the butter and remaining sugar until light and fluffy. Then beat in the melted chocolate and the nut mixture; mix well to combine. Cover and refrigerate for 2 hours.

Shape teaspoonfuls of the dough into crescents and place onto baking sheets spaced 5 cm (2 inches) apart. Bake for 15 to 20 minutes. Transfer to a wire rack to cool completely.

Melt the remaining chocolate in a bowl set over a heavy saucepan of barely simmering water. Remove from the heat. Dip one end of the biscuit into the chocolate or drizzle with a thin stream of chocolate. Return to the wire rack and allow the chocolate to set. Once set, store in airtight containers. Not suitable for freezing.

Double Chocolate Chip Muffins

These rich, chocolate muffins make a great morning snack with a cappuccino or glass of cold milk.

MAKES 10

280 g (10 oz) plain flour
40 g (1½ oz) unsweetened cocoa powder
1 Tbsp baking powder
½ tsp salt
110 g (4 oz) sugar
85 g (3 oz) semisweet chocolate chips and
   40 g (1½ oz) white chocolate chips
2 eggs
8 Tbsp sunflower or vegetable oil
230 ml (8 fl oz) milk
1 tsp vanilla extract

Preheat oven to 200°C/400°F/Gas 6. Line a 10-cup muffin pan with double-paper cases. Half fill any remaining empty cups in the pan with water to prevent them from scorching. Sieve the flour, cocoa powder, baking powder and salt into a bowl. Stir in the sugar and chocolate chips, then make a well in the centre.

In another bowl beat the eggs with the oil until foamy. Gradually beat in the milk and vanilla extract. Pour into the well and stir until just combined. Do not overmix; the batter should be slightly lumpy.

Spoon the batter into the prepared cups, filling each about three quarters full. Bake until risen, golden and springy when pressed with your fingertip, about 20 minutes. Remove the pan to a wire rack to cool, about 2 minutes, then remove the muffins to the rack to cool completely. The muffins can be served warm or at room temperature.

Chocolate Chip & Coffee Shortbreads

Always make shortbread with butter for the best flavour.

MAKES ABOUT **20**

170 g (6 oz) butter, plus extra for greasing
200 g (7 oz) plain flour
2 tsp instant coffee granules
55 g (2 oz) icing sugar, sieved
Few drops of vanilla extract
85 g (3 oz) small chocolate chips

Cream the butter until soft, then gradually work in all the remaining ingredients except the chocolate. Continue working the dough until it begins to come together, then add the chocolate and knead into a firm dough. Shape into a roll about 40 cm (15 inches) long, then cover in clingfilm and chill for about 1 hour.

Preheat the oven to 180°C/350°F/Gas 4 and lightly grease two baking sheets. Slice the dough into about 20 pieces, then place on the baking sheets and flatten slightly with a fork. Bake the shortbreads in the preheated oven for 20 to 25 minutes, until lightly golden.

Allow the shortbreads to cool for 1 to 2 minutes on the baking sheets, then transfer them carefully with a palette knife to a wire rack until completely cold. Store in an airtight tin.

Florentines

*These rich and sophisticated biscuits
have always been a favourite.*

MAKES ABOUT 16

6 glacé cherries, rinsed and chopped
100 g (3½ oz) mixed chopped peel
110 g (4 oz) roughly chopped mixed nuts
1 Tbsp plain flour
3 Tbsp butter
55 g (2 oz) caster sugar
4 Tbsp single cream
55 g (2 oz) bittersweet chocolate, broken into squares
1 tsp coffee extract

Preheat the oven to 180°C/350°F/Gas 4. Line two heavy baking sheets with baking parchment.

Mix the fruit and nuts together and chop them finely, then toss them in the flour. Heat the butter, sugar and cream together until the butter has melted, then bring just to the boil. Add the prepared fruits, and stir well.

Place spoonfuls of mixture on the baking sheets, allowing room for them to spread. Bake for 15 to 20 minutes, until golden. Cool slightly, then transfer to a wire rack to cool completely.

Melt the chocolate (see page 12). Stir in the coffee extract. Spread a little of the chocolate thinly over the back of each florentine, then leave them face down on the wire rack to set.

COOKIES

Chocolate Viennese Whirls

A rich and attractive biscuit, perfect for an afternoon tea party.

MAKES ABOUT **20**

170 g (6 oz) butter
55 g (2 oz) icing sugar
225 g (8 oz) plain flour
½ tsp vanilla extract
10 candied cherries, halved
250 g (9 oz) semisweet chocolate, coarsely chopped

Preheat oven to 170°C/325°F/Gas 3. Grease two baking sheets. Beat together the butter and sugar until light and fluffy. Sieve the flour into the bowl, add the vanilla and mix well to combine.

Spoon the mixture into a pastry bag fitted with a large star-shaped tube. Pipe flat whirls onto the baking sheets. Put half a cherry on each one. Bake for 20 minutes until just golden. Leave to cool on the baking sheets for 5 minutes, then transfer to a wire rack to cool completely.

Meanwhile, melt the chocolate in a small bowl set over a heavy saucepan of simmering water (see page 12). When the biscuits are completely cold, dip the bottoms into the melted chocolate. Return to the wire rack (chocolate-side up) until the chocolate is set. Once completely set, store in an airtight container.

White Chocolate & Cashew Thins

These cookies are really thin and crunchy. Try eating them with ice cream.

MAKES ABOUT **30**

4 Tbsp slightly salted butter, softened
40 g (1½ oz) packed light brown sugar
4 Tbsp golden syrup
55 g (2 oz) salted cashews, finely chopped
45 g (1¾ oz) plain flour
1 tsp vanilla essence
250 g (9 oz) white chocolate, coarsely chopped

Preheat oven to 180°C/350°F/Gas 4. Grease two baking sheets. In a heavy saucepan, melt the butter. Add the brown sugar and golden syrup, then bring to the boil stirring continuously for 3 to 4 minutes until the sugar dissolves. Remove from the heat. Stir in the cashews, flour and vanilla until well mixed.

Drop half-teaspoon mounds spaced well apart onto the baking sheets. Use the back of a spoon to spread each mound into a circle. Bake for 8 to 10 minutes or until golden brown. Turn the baking sheets around halfway through cooking. Cool on the baking sheets for 1 minute, then transfer to a wire rack to cool completely.

Melt the chocolate in a small bowl set over a saucepan of barely simmering water (see page 12). Dip a fork into the melted chocolate and drizzle over the cookies. Return to the wire rack to set. Once set, store in an airtight container. Not suitable for freezing.

Tip

- *Do not overbake these cookies or they may be too dry and taste stale. Because they are thin, they continue to bake even when removed from the oven.*

Chocolate Pinwheels

A good, fun biscuit that's great for kids' parties.

MAKES ABOUT **25**

8 Tbsp butter, softened
70 g (2½ oz) caster sugar
1 egg, beaten
1 tsp vanilla extract
200 g (7 oz) plain flour
Pinch of salt
25 g (1 oz) semisweet chocolate

In a large bowl beat together the butter and sugar until light and fluffy. Beat in the egg and vanilla until blended. Sieve the flour and salt onto this mixture; beat briefly until combined.

Divide the dough in half and wrap one half in clingfilm. Refrigerate until firm enough to roll (about 1 hour). Melt the chocolate in a small bowl set over a heavy saucepan of simmering water (see page 12). Allow to cool slightly. Add the melted chocolate to the remaining dough and mix until completely blended. Wrap the chocolate dough in clingfilm and refrigerate until firm enough to roll.

On a lightly floured surface, roll the vanilla dough into a rectangle. Repeat with the chocolate dough, rolling to the same size. Place the chocolate dough on top of the plain dough. Roll up the dough, from one short end, as tightly as possible. Wrap in clingfilm tightly and refrigerate until very firm.

Preheat oven to 190°C/375°F/Gas 5. Grease two baking sheets. Using a sharp knife, cut the dough roll into 6-mm (¼-inch) slices and place well apart on the baking sheets. Bake for 7 to 10 minutes until beginning to change colour at the edges. Transfer to a wire rack to cool completely. Store in an airtight container.

Almond & Chocolate Clusters

A light nutty cookie that you can either dip or drizzle with chocolate.

MAKES ABOUT **22**

8 Tbsp butter, softened
150 g (5½ oz) caster sugar
1 egg
½ tsp almond extract
25 g (1 oz) ground blanched almonds
200 g (7 oz) plain flour
110 g (4 oz) slivered almonds

TOPPING
4 Tbsp double cream
170 g (6 oz) semisweet chocolate chips
2 tsp golden syrup

Preheat oven to 180°C/350°F/Gas 4. Grease two baking sheets. Beat together the butter and sugar until well blended. Add the egg and almond extract; beat until light and fluffy. Then add the ground almonds and flour. Stir until just combined. Form the dough into walnut-sized balls and roll in the slivered almonds, pressing down slightly to coat each ball thoroughly.

Place the balls on the baking sheets spaced 5 cm (2 inches) apart. Bake for 15 minutes. Transfer the cookies to a cool, flat surface covered with greaseproof paper.

Meanwhile, heat the cream, but do not allow to boil. Remove from the heat and stir in the chocolate chips and golden syrup. Cover and allow to stand for 10 minutes. Mix the glaze gently with a wooden spoon until smooth.

When the cookies are cool, drizzle patterns on them with the warm chocolate or dip each cookie into the chocolate. Return the cookies to the greaseproof paper and place in the refrigerator until set. Once set, store in an airtight container. These cookies are best eaten soon after decorating as they contain fresh cream; however, they may be stored for up to 2 days in the refrigerator.

Chocolate Wafers

These thin, nutty wafers are great served with ice cream.

MAKES ABOUT **28**

8 Tbsp butter, softened
55 g (2 oz) caster sugar
8 Tbsp golden syrup
1 egg
½ tsp vanilla essence
170 g (6 oz) plain flour
1 Tbsp unsweetened cocoa powder
¼ tsp baking soda
85 g (3 oz) chopped mixed nuts

Preheat oven to 180°C/350°F/Gas 4. Line two baking sheets with non-stick baking parchment.

Beat the butter, sugar and syrup together until light and fluffy. Thoroughly beat in the egg and vanilla. Sieve the flour, cocoa and baking soda onto the butter mixture. Lightly stir into the mixture with the chopped mixed nuts.

Place walnut-sized spoonfuls spaced 5 cm (2 inches) apart onto the baking sheets. Bake for 15 minutes. Lift from the baking sheet with a thin metal spatula and lay over a lightly oiled rolling pin to produce a curved shape. Leave to cool on the rolling pin for a few minutes before transferring to a wire rack to cool completely. Store in an airtight container.

Chocolate Wafers

Mocha Chunk Cookies

A classic, chunky-style cookie with a rich coffee taste.

MAKES ABOUT 16

200 g (7 oz) plain flour
2 Tbsp unsweetened cocoa powder
¼ tsp baking soda
Pinch of salt
2 tsp instant coffee granules
1 tsp coffee liqueur (optional)
110 g (4 oz) caster sugar
55 g (2 oz) packed dark brown sugar
8 Tbsp slightly salted butter, softened
1 egg
340 g (12 oz) semisweet chocolate, coarsely chopped

Preheat oven to 180°C/350°F/Gas 4. Grease two baking sheets. In a medium-sized bowl, sieve the flour, cocoa, baking soda and salt. In a small bowl, dissolve the coffee granules in coffee liqueur or hot water; set aside. In a large bowl, mix together the sugars. Add the butter and mix thoroughly until light. Add the egg and coffee mixture and beat until smooth. Then add the flour mixture and chocolate chunks. Mix gently with a spoon until well combined.

Place rounded tablespoons of the mixture on the baking sheets, spaced 5 cm (2 inches) apart. Bake for 20 minutes until set. Transfer the cookies to a flat surface to cool. Once completely cool, store in an airtight container.

Chocolate Fudge Cookies

These cookies have a pure chocolate taste and a wonderfully smooth texture.

MAKES ABOUT **28**

250 g (9 oz) semisweet chocolate, finely chopped
200 g (7 oz) plain flour
25 g (1 oz) unsweetened cocoa powder
½ tsp baking powder
Pinch of salt

8 Tbsp butter, softened
225 g (8 oz) packed dark brown sugar
2 eggs
1 tsp vanilla extract
125 g (4½ oz) white chocolate, coarsely chopped

Preheat oven to 150°C/300°F/Gas 2. Grease two baking sheets. Melt the chocolate in a bowl set over a heavy saucepan of simmering water (see page 12). Set aside to cool slightly.

Sieve the flour, cocoa, baking powder and salt; set aside. In a separate bowl, beat the butter and sugar together until light and fluffy. Beat in the eggs and vanilla until well blended. Mix in the cooled chocolate and fold in the flour until just combined.

Drop rounded tablespoonfuls of the dough spaced 5 cm (2 inches) apart onto the baking sheets. Bake for 18 to 20 minutes. Cool the cookies on the sheet for one minute, then transfer to a wire rack to cool completely.

Meanwhile, melt the white chocolate in a small bowl set over a heavy saucepan of barely simmering water (see page 12). When the cookies are completely cool, dip a fork into the melted chocolate and drizzle over the cookies. Return to the wire rack until the chocolate is set. Once completely set, store in an airtight container.

Tip

• *Keep a batch of these cookies in the freezer as they're quick to thaw at short notice. Place a sheet of greaseproof paper between each layer and place in heavy-duty freezer bags or small airtight containers, expelling as much air as possible. Defrost in their wrappings for between 15 to 20 minutes.*

Chocolate-Dipped Orange Shortbread

These elegant piped biscuits make a great addition to an afternoon tea.

MAKES ABOUT **35**

400 g (14 oz) plain flour
Pinch of salt
1 tsp baking powder
225 g (8 oz) butter, softened
225 g (8 oz) granulated sugar
1 egg
1 tsp grated orange zest
170 g (6 oz) semisweet chocolate, chopped

Preheat oven to 180°C/350°F/Gas 4. Grease two baking sheets. Combine the flour, salt and baking powder in a bowl. Beat the butter and sugar in a large bowl until light and fluffy. Beat in the egg and orange zest. Fold in the flour until just combined.

Spoon the mixture into a pastry bag fitted with a large star tube. Pipe 3.75-cm (1½-inch) strips, spaced 5 cm (2 inches) apart onto the baking sheets. Bake for 10 to 12 minutes until just beginning to turn light golden around the edges. Carefully transfer to a wire rack to cool completely.

Melt the chocolate in a small bowl over a heavy saucepan of barely simmering water (see page 12). Dip the top of each biscuit into the melted chocolate. Place the biscuits on a wire rack until the chocolate is set. Once completely cool, store in an airtight container.

FROM THE REFRIGERATOR

Rich Mocha Refrigerator Cake

This delicious dessert cake is based on an Italian recipe. It combines the strong taste of espresso coffee with the sweetness of chocolate.

SERVES **8**

225 g (8 oz) dark chocolate, broken into small pieces

2 Tbsp instant espresso

6 Tbsp hot water

3 Tbsp Tia Maria or other coffee liqueur

225 g (8 oz) unsalted butter

2 Tbsp caster sugar

2 eggs, separated (see page 4)

110 g (4 oz) roughly chopped blanched almonds

12 petit beurre biscuits, cut cleanly into halves

Icing sugar (optional)

Line a 900-g (2-pound) loaf tin with non-stick baking parchment. Melt the chocolate in a large bowl over hot water or in a microwave (see page 12). Dissolve the instant espresso in the hot water, then add it to the melted chocolate with the liqueur. Stir until thoroughly blended. Leave to cool slightly.

Beat the butter in a bowl until soft, then add the sugar and egg yolks, one at a time. Stir in the almonds and cooled chocolate. Whisk the egg whites until stiff, then fold them into the mixture. Carefully add the biscuit halves one at a time, tossing them gently until they are coated with chocolate. Make sure they remain separate and do not stick together.

Carefully spoon the mixture into the prepared tin, pressing down lightly to ensure there are no gaps, but avoid breaking the biscuits. Try to ensure that the biscuits are evenly distributed throughout the loaf. Chill for at least 2 hours.

To serve, turn the loaf out onto a serving plate and remove the paper. Sprinkle with sieved icing sugar, if you wish, and serve in slices. Keep the cake chilled until you are ready to serve.

Tip

- *This cake is very rich and should be served with just a small dollop of sweetened yoghurt. Omit the eggs if you prefer, for a slightly heavier cake, which is still utterly delicious.*

Chocolate Fudge Ripple

Deliciously fun ice cream that looks and tastes divine.

SERVES **4** TO **6**

4 large egg yolks (see page 4)
110 g (4 oz) caster sugar
284 ml (½ pt) milk
½ tsp vanilla extract
284 ml (½ pt) double cream

CHOCOLATE FUDGE SAUCE
110 g (4 oz) dark chocolate, broken into small pieces
3 Tbsp golden syrup
2 Tbsp hot water
1 tsp coffee essence or strong instant coffee (optional)

Use the method for making the basic ice-cream mixture (see page 43) to prepare a custard using the eggs, sugar and milk. Let cool completely, then add the vanilla and cream, and chill.

Prepare the sauce while the custard is cooling. Using a small, heavy-bottomed saucepan, melt the chocolate with the syrup, water and coffee essence, if using (see page 12). Remove from the heat as soon as the chocolate has melted, then beat thoroughly. Let cool, then chill until required.

Freeze-churn the ice cream until ready to serve. Pack spoonfuls of the finished ice cream into a suitable freezer container, drizzling or spooning the sauce randomly over the scoops. Harden the ice cream in the freezer before serving, or store until required.

Double Chocolate Chip Ice Cream

Use the best chocolate you can find since this will improve both the flavour and the texture.

SERVES **4** TO **6**

1 large or 2 small cinnamon sticks
284 ml (½ pt) single cream
4 large egg yolks (see page 4)
70 g (2½ oz) brown sugar
170 g (6 oz) chocolate, finely chopped
284 ml (½ pt) double cream
85 g (3 oz) chocolate, roughly chopped

Heat the cinnamon stick(s) with the single cream until almost boiling. Cover the pan and leave to infuse for 20 minutes. Remove the sticks.

Whisk together the egg yolks and sugar until thick and slightly paler in colour. Reheat the cream until almost boiling, then add the finely chopped chocolate and stir until it has melted completely. Pour the mixture onto the eggs, stirring continuously, then heat gently over a pan of hot (but not boiling) water for 3 to 4 minutes, until slightly thickened. Do not heat this mixture in a saucepan over direct heat, since the chocolate may cause it to burn.

Cool the custard, and then chill it lightly for 30 to 40 minutes; it will become very thick. Lightly whip the double cream, fold it into the chilled custard and freeze-churn the mixture. Add the chopped chocolate once the cream has thickened in the ice-cream machine, then continue churning until it is ready to serve.

Chocolate Kumquat Gelato

Italian gelatos are often vibrantly fruity. Kumquats are widely available year-round in most supermarkets.

SERVES **4** TO **6**

40 g (1½ oz) unsweetened cocoa powder, sieved
450 ml (16 fl oz) cold milk
1 large or 2 small cinnamon sticks
70 g (2½ oz) sugar
4 large egg yolks, beaten (see page 4)
1 Tbsp coffee essence, or strong instant coffee
225 g (8 oz) kumquats

Blend the cocoa to a smooth, thin paste with some of the milk, then mix it with the remaining milk in a heavy saucepan. Heat the milk with the cinnamon and sugar, stirring until the sugar has dissolved.

Beat the egg yolks with the coffee essence until slightly thickened and pale in colour; pour on the hot milk, beating all the time. Rinse the saucepan with cold water, return the mixture to it, and heat gently. Stir constantly, until the mixture has thickened sufficiently to just coat the back of a wooden spoon. Remove from the heat, allow the custard to cool completely, then remove the cinnamon stick(s).

Wash the kumquats and process them until finely chopped; pieces of peel should still be obvious, but not too large. Mix the kumquats with the cooled chocolate mixture, then turn into the ice-cream machine and freeze-churn until ready to serve.

Tip

• *Although kumquats are a great fruit to use in this recipe because of their year-round availability, other dessert fruits would work well too. Try apricots, peaches, nectarines or clementines.*

White Chocolate Chunk Ice Cream

White chocolate is much sweeter than semisweet or dark chocolate, so less sugar is used in this recipe. The basic mixture is flavoured with white chocolate, and chips of white and dark chocolate are added at the end.

SERVES **4** TO **6**

570 ml (1 pt) milk
55 g (2 oz) caster sugar
125 g (4½ oz) white chocolate, roughly chopped
1 tsp vanilla extract
Pinch of salt
55 g (2 oz) white chocolate chips, coarsely chopped
40 g (1½ oz) dark chocolate chips, coarsely chopped

Heat the milk until almost boiling, when tiny bubbles begin to rise to the surface. Add the sugar and white chocolate. Stir until the sugar has dissolved and the chocolate has melted, then leave the milk to cool completely.

Next, stir the vanilla and salt into the cold milk, then turn into the ice-cream machine. Freeze-churn until the mixture is thick, then add the roughly chopped chocolate chips and continue churning until ready to serve.

Double Chocolate Peppermint Ice Cream

A chocolate and peppermint treat that can be made even more special by adding 1 to 2 tablespoons crème de menthe, if you wish.

SERVES **4** TO **6**

40 g (1½ oz) unsweetened cocoa powder, sieved
150 g (5½ oz) caster sugar
570 ml (1 pt) cold milk
1 tsp vanilla extract
1 to 2 Tbsp crème de menthe (optional)
85 g (3 oz) peppermint creams, chopped
40 g (1½ oz) chocolate chips, coarsely chopped

Blend the cocoa and sugar together to a thin paste with a little of the cold milk, then add the remaining milk. Heat until almost boiling, then add the vanilla extract. Stir until the sugar is almost dissolved. Leave the milk to cool completely, then add the crème de menthe, if desired.

Freeze-churn until thick, then add the chopped peppermint creams and the chocolate chips. Continue to churn until the ice cream is ready to serve.

Mexican Chocolate Ice Cream

Strongly flavoured with cinnamon, this is an ideal dessert to serve with an exotic fruit salad or fresh sliced papaya.

SERVES **4** TO **6**

40 g (1½ oz) unsweetened cocoa powder, sieved
150 g (5½ oz) caster sugar
570 ml (1 pt) cold milk
2 large cinnamon sticks
1 large egg white (see page 4)
40 g (1½ oz) pecans, chopped

Blend the cocoa and sugar to a thin paste with a little of the cold milk. Whisk in the remaining milk, then heat gently with the cinnamon sticks until the sugar has dissolved. Remove the saucepan from the heat and leave until completely cold. Discard the cinnamon.

Lightly beat the egg white until very frothy, then add the cold milk. Turn into the ice-cream machine and freeze-churn until almost ready to serve. Add the chopped pecans and continue churning for a few more minutes.

Mexican Chocolate Ice Cream

Mississippi Mud Pie

SERVES **8**

22 crushed digestive biscuits

Large knob of butter, melted

110 g (4 oz) plain chocolate, melted

1.1 L (2 pt) coffee ice cream

1.1 L (2 pt) chocolate ice cream

2 Tbsp Tia Maria

2 Tbsp brandy

DECORATION

Whipped cream

Grated chocolate

Put the crumbs, butter and chocolate into a bowl and mix well together. Press the crumbs firmly and evenly over the bottom and sides of a greased 23-cm (9-inch) flan dish. Chill.

Allow the ice creams to soften slightly. Put in a bowl and add the Tia Maria and brandy. Blend well together. Spoon the ice cream into the chocolate case and put in the freezer until solid.

Remove the pie from the freezer about 15 minutes before serving. Decorate with whipped cream and grated chocolate.

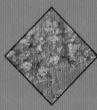

SUBLIME DESSERTS

Chocolate–Coffee Mousse

Quick and easy to make, this light dessert can be prepared in advance.

SERVES **8**

500 ml (18 fl oz) double strength cold coffee
   (add 2 Tbsp instant espresso to ordinary cold coffee
   to get the right flavour)
1 Tbsp gelatine
3 Tbsp boiling water
85 g (3 oz) dark chocolate
3 eggs, separated (see page 4)
70 g (2½ oz) caster sugar
280 ml (½ pt) double cream
2 Tbsp good-quality cocoa powder
Grated bittersweet or semisweet chocolate,
   to decorate

Mix the instant espresso into the cold coffee. Sprinkle gelatine over the boiling water, stir well, then leave for 3 to 4 minutes to dissolve completely.

Melt the chocolate. Whisk together the egg yolks and sugar until pale and thick, then gradually whisk in the cold coffee and fold in the melted chocolate. Stir the gelatine to check that it has completely dissolved, then blend 1 or 2 spoonfuls of the coffee mixture into the gelatine (this helps it to blend into the mousse more easily). Fold the gelatine into the coffee mixture.

Lightly whip the cream until thick and soft, fold in the cocoa powder and then fold this mixture into the coffee mixture. Pour the mousse into a glass bowl. Whisk the egg whites until stiff and fold in. Chill for at least 2 hours until set. Sprinkle with grated chocolate before serving.

Chocolate Chip & Peanut Butter Bread

This is a moist, dense bread with a good, peanutty flavour. The chocolate crumb topping is partly layered into the mixture for an extra-rich chocolate taste.

MAKES **8** TO **10** SERVINGS

340 g (12 oz) plain flour

2 tsp baking powder

¼ tsp salt

170 g (6 oz) dark chocolate chips

170 ml (6 fl oz) smooth or chunky peanut butter,
   at room temperature

1 Tbsp sugar

1 egg, lightly beaten (see
   page 4)

230 ml (8 fl oz) milk

1 tsp vanilla extract

CHOCOLATE CRUMB TOPPING

110 g (4 oz) sugar

25 g (1 oz) unsweetened cocoa powder

3 Tbsp unsalted butter, cut into pieces

2 Tbsp finely chopped, dry-roasted peanuts

Preheat oven to 180°C/350°F/Gas 4. Lightly grease a 23 × 13-cm (9 × 5-inch) loaf tin. Sieve the flour, baking powder and salt into a large bowl. Stir in the chocolate chips and make a well in the centre. Put the peanut butter into another bowl and beat with an electric mixer to break up and soften. Gradually beat in the sugar, egg, milk and vanilla extract. Pour into the well and lightly stir with a fork until combined.

Combine the crumb topping ingredients in a small bowl. Spoon half the loaf mixture into the prepared tin and smooth, sprinkling with half of the crumb mixture. Spoon the remaining loaf mixture into the tin. Gently smooth the top and sprinkle with the remaining crumb mixture. With a round-bladed knife or spoon handle, gently draw through the mixture in a zigzag pattern to give the mixture a slight marbling.

Bake the bread until risen and golden, and a fine skewer inserted into the centre comes out clean, 50 to 55 minutes. Cool in the tin on a wire rack for about 25 minutes, then carefully turn out onto a wire rack, top-side up. Cool completely, then wrap and keep for a day before serving, if possible.

Tiramisu

This is a classic Italian coffee trifle, garnished with dark chocolate.

SERVES **4** TO **6**

8 Tbsp hot water

4 Tbsp coarsely ground Italian-roast coffee

3 egg yolks (see page 4)

225 g (8 oz) mascarpone cheese

3 Tbsp orange liqueur

12 Italian sponge fingers

55 g (2 oz) finely chopped or grated dark chocolate

Pour the hot water over the coffee then leave to stand for 10 minutes. Strain the coffee through a fine sieve, then leave until completely cold.

Beat the egg yolks in a bowl, then add the mascarpone cheese and beat until smooth. Add 1 tablespoon of the orange liqueur and beat again. Add the remaining liqueur to the cold coffee.

Dip the sponge fingers into the coffee as you use them to line the base of a trifle dish and top with the custard, or arrange them in layers with the custard in wine glasses. Sprinkle with chocolate just before serving.

Serving Idea

• *Serve in one large dish or layered in wine glasses–this is an attractive way to present this dessert at a dinner party.*

Tiramisu

Chocolate Waffles

A delicious dessert that can also be served for elevenses.

SERVES **4**

40 g (1½ oz) plain flour
2 Tbsp unsweetened cocoa powder
Pinch salt
2 tsp baking powder
2 Tbsp sugar
2 eggs, separated
280 ml (½ pt) milk
4 Tbsp butter, melted
Chocolate Syrup (purchased or see page 19), maple
　　syrup and 55 g (2 oz) pecans, chopped, to serve

🍫　Sift together the flour, cocoa powder, salt and baking powder. Stir in the sugar. Make a well in the centre and add the egg yolks, milk and melted butter. Stir well.

🍫　Whisk the egg whites until stiff and fold them lightly into the batter. Pour the batter into a heated waffle iron and cook until golden.

🍫　To serve, mix together the two syrups and stir in the nuts. Serve the waffles immediately with the sauce poured over the top.

Chocolate Soufflés

In this recipe, baked pastry cases hold the chocolate soufflé mixture instead of ramekins.

SERVES **6** TO **8**

6 to 8 brioche moulds or other deep tartlet pans, buttered and lined with Chocolate Pastry (see page 22), baked blind
170 g (6 oz) semisweet chocolate, chopped
4 Tbsp butter
4 eggs, separated
2 Tbsp brandy or Cognac
¼ tsp baking soda
2 Tbsp sugar
Icing sugar, for dusting

Preheat oven to 220°C/425°F/Gas 7. Set the moulds or tartlet pans on a baking sheet for easier handling. In a heavy saucepan over low heat, melt the chocolate and butter until smooth, stirring frequently. Remove from the heat and beat in the egg yolks, one at a time, then beat in the brandy; set aside.

In a large bowl, beat the egg whites and baking soda until soft peaks form. Sprinkle in the sugar, 1 tablespoon at a time, and continue beating until soft peaks form again.

Stir a spoonful of whites into the chocolate mixture to lighten it, then fold in the remaining whites. Divide the mixture evenly among the moulds or tartlet pans, filling them almost to the pastry edge. Bake for 10 to 12 minutes until the mixture is just set, but still slightly wobbly. Dust with icing sugar and serve immediately.

Chocolate Truffle Tartlets

These tartlets are deliciously indulgent. Experiment with different liqueurs to vary the flavour of this recipe.

MAKES **24**

340 g (12 oz) prepared shortcrust pastry
225 g (8 oz) dark chocolate
230 ml (8 fl oz) double cream
2 Tbsp brandy
1 Tbsp grated orange zest
Icing sugar, for dusting

Preheat oven to 200°C/400°F/Gas 6. Line the cups in the muffin tin with pastry, prick the bases and bake for 12 to 15 minutes or until cooked. Leave to cool.

Meanwhile, in a heavy saucepan, heat the chocolate, cream and brandy together. Stir until smooth. Stir in the orange zest and chill until thick. Whisk the mixture until fluffy and use to fill the pastry cases.

To serve, dust each of the tartlets with sieved icing sugar.

Devil's Food Cake

Quite simply a chocolate classic, this delicious cake is enjoyed by chocoholics worldwide.

SERVES 10 TO 12

85 g (3 oz) semisweet chocolate, chopped
55 g (2 oz) cocoa powder
400 g (14 oz) plain flour
2 tsp baking soda
½ tsp salt
8 Tbsp unsalted butter, softened
500 g (1 lb 2 oz) brown sugar
1 Tbsp vanilla extract

3 eggs
170 ml (6 fl oz) soured cream
1 tsp vinegar
230 ml (8 fl oz) boiling water

CHOCOLATE FROSTING

680 ml (1¼ pt) whipping cream
1 kg (2¼ lb) semisweet chocolate, chopped
1 Tbsp vanilla extract

Preheat oven to 190°C/375°F/Gas 5. Butter two 23-cm (9-inch) round cake tins, 3.75 cm (1½ inches) deep. Line the bases with greaseproof paper; butter the paper and flour the pans.

Melt the chocolate (see page 12), stirring frequently until smooth. Set aside. Sift together the cocoa, flour, baking soda and salt. Cream the butter, brown sugar and vanilla extract until light and creamy, about 5 minutes, scraping the sides of the bowl occasionally. Add the eggs, one at a time, beating well after each addition. Add the flour mixture alternately with the soured cream in three batches, beating until well blended. Stir in the vinegar and the melted chocolate and slowly beat in the boiling water; the batter will be thin. Pour into the tins.

Bake for 20 to 25 minutes until a fine skewer inserted into the centre comes out with just a few crumbs attached. Cool the cakes in the tins on a wire rack. Remove the cakes from the tins, remove from the paper and allow to cool on the rack.

Meanwhile prepare the frosting. In a heavy saucepan over medium heat, bring the cream to the boil. Remove from the heat and stir in the chocolate all at once until melted and smooth. Add the vanilla extract and allow to cool slightly. Pour into a large bowl and refrigerate for 1 hour, stirring twice until the frosting is a spreading consistency.

Slice each cake layer horizontally into two layers. Place one layer cut-side up on a plate and spread with one-sixth of the frosting. Add a layer on top and cover with another sixth of frosting. Continue layering in this way and place the fourth layer rounded side up. Frost the top and sides of the cake and serve at room temperature.

Index

index